Secrets of the East African Wilderness

Secrets of the East African Wilderness

G Malinga

To order additional copies of this book, contact:
Xlibris Corporation
0-800-644-6988
www.xlibrispublishing.co.uk
Orders@xlibrispublishing.co.uk
301360

CONTENTS

DISCLAIMER

Some of the experiences narrated in this book though real have not been scientifically proven. The author is not therefore liable for any suit arising from the application of these experiences to real life. The narratives should be treated primarily for their literary value.

Enjoy your reading.

PREFACE

This is a short narrative of the East African wilderness experience in the olden days. Most of the descriptions given here are first hand reports that were passed on as valuable oral possessions of the community to its younger generation and are essentially true accounts of humans interacting with animals either for food, defense or a shared habitat.

ACKNOWLEDGEMENTS

I am greatly indebted to Dr. Dan Kasule of the Centre for Academic Development, Dr. Nana Adu-Pipim Boaduo and Dr. Moumakwa of the department of Languages and Social Sciences Education of the University of Botswana for reading the original draft manuscript and providing useful insights and suggestions. Also my sincere thanks to Prof. Kezilahabi of the department of African Languages and Literature, University of Botswana. All colleagues who read through the draft manuscript and made useful suggestions are duly acknowledged.

CHAPTER 1

Discovery of a Cure for Snake Bite

When you happen to meet two snakes fighting, the gods may have actually smiled at you! Medicine men in the Eastern region of Uganda crafted their snakebite healing trade by sheer coincidence. In those days young men and boys often herded the family livestock. Each morning they took the livestock to graze only returning late each evening to bring back the herds to the homestead where a kraal had been constructed to keep the animals safely for the night.

During the day's expedition by the herdsmen and herd boys a lot of events that sometimes significantly changed their lives took place. Among these was the frequent encounter with wild animals usually predators such as lions, leopards, buffalos and a variety of reptiles. These animals had to be waded off in order to protect livestock. The only weapons available then were spears, swords and clubs. The habitat was sparsely populated by people and this provided a haven for animals to freely roam the vast uninhabited terrain without fear of harassment.

However, for herd boys and herdsmen it was not uncommon to meet rare occurrences like a snake fight in the open savannah. This was a sanctimonious event because it promised a recipe for the discovery of a remedy for snake poison. In those days hospitals were a long way away from people and science had not developed as it is now. When one was bitten by a snake it resulted in certain death.

Snakes were a common sight to the humans firstly because of the vast territory available as a natural habitat for the snakes and secondly because the ecosystem of humans was directly linked to that of the snakes. For instance water was only obtainable from natural wells, rivers, swamps and lakes and this was the very place the snakes also visited to quench their thirst. Furthermore human activities always involved bush trips: either to hunt, pick fruits, collect firewood, fetch water, tend livestock or simply travel to visit other relatives in distant locations. This invariably increased the chances of meeting snakes moving about in the vicinity.

Livestock have well developed senses for spotting snakes. When livestock spot a snake in the vicinity they generally encircle the snake whilst standing alert facing the direction of the snake with ears raised high. Any attempt by the trapped snake to fight back results in a stampede designed to kill the snake, which usually flees from the herd.

When two snakes fight the battle is a 'do or die' affair that lasts several hours. The interesting part of this fight is that when the snakes fight fatal injuries occur all the time. One snake will ultimately bite the other snake spewing deadly poison through its fangs and resulting in fatally injuring it. When this occurs a miracle happens and only science may perhaps provide an adequate explanation for this observation. The attacker snake would quickly rush off to the bush to look for a plant remedy that it brings back and administers on the victim thus reviving it. No sooner does this happen than the fight resumed until another fatal injury occurred resulting in the attacker snake rushing off again to bring back and administer the plant remedy to the injured snake. This would go on and on for a very long time until a truce was declared by the two warring snakes.

As herd boys or herdsmen if you chanced to witness this battle of the snakes it was expected that you had to tread carefully and watch attentively until you traced and spotted the exact plant remedy that the attacker snake brought to revive its victim. This, however, was a dangerous task, because once any of the warring snakes discovered that there was an intruder around they would stop fighting. Instead they would turn all their energies on the intruder and give chase with serious consequences.

Strangely, knowledge of this remedy appears to be the snakes' guarded secret, since anyone deemed by the snake to be prying when the remedy was being collected and administered had to be eliminated by all means. Therefore, the elders' advice was that when you meet two snakes fighting look for the best vantage position such as the top of an anthill or quietly climb a nearby tree and try to locate the life giving plant remedy. Once you located the plant remedy by observing the snake's errand, you became the village's snakebite healer for that particular species of snakebite. Your knowledge became a guarded secret, only handed down to one of your children at the time of your imminent death at old age and this would be passed on to subsequent generations.

This knowledge brought instant wealth and prominence to the family because anyone bitten by a snake within the surrounding villages sought help from the snakebite healer. The charges were dependent upon the severity of the attack. This was usually determined by how big or lethal the snake was and payment ranged from a cock to a he-goat. However, other benefits included donations from crop harvests, and invitations to attend family feasts.

Usually the area of the body prone to snake bites is the leg below the knee. Snakebites are lethal and usually result in immediate death because the poison is carried by the blood vessels to the heart. When bitten by a snake the first course of action is to seek treatment by calling out for immediate assistance. It is also important to note the type of snake that has bitten you. It is said that for some snake species once it has bitten you any further bites are not fatal save for the deadly fangs because the poison has all been used up in the first bite.

The second course of action when bitten by a snake is to try and reduce the amount of poison circulating in the body. This involves using any sharp instrument to make small incisions around the area of the snakebite. This causes deliberate bleeding which would drain much of the poison from the blood stream. In the absence of a sharp instrument a friend without cracks in his or her mouth could suck out and spit the blood from the area punctured. This action delays the poison reaching the human heart.

When much of the poison has been drained, a mopping up operation is then carried out. This is where the medicine men come in handy. When the medicine men are consulted, they administer the anti-snake bite remedy to the patient by rubbing the raw plant remedy to the wound. This serves to neutralize the effect of the poison. Like the snake poison, the anti-snake bite remedy is also carried by the blood vessels around the entire body.

Questions

1. Why was it common for people to meet snakes in the past?
2. Describe how snakebite medicine was discovered in the past.
3. Explain the steps that were taken when one was bitten by a snake.
4. What were the benefits of knowing snakebite medicine?
5. Narrate what happens when two snakes fight.
6. Dramatize a snake fight.

New Words			
habitat	errand	kraal	recipe
remedy	fangs	expedition	truce
casualties	reptiles	stampede	sanctimonious
prying	fatal	ecosystem	significantly
vantage	intruder	lethal	coincidence
imminent	incisions	neutralize	revive

CHAPTER 2

A Snake and Its Enemies

Some snakes are gigantic and long whilst others are small yet adapted to their environment. A speed race with them in the open grassland is a big gamble for any daring opponent. However there are two known small animals that have the audacity to challenge a snake into a fight no matter its size. One such animal is the slow moving chameleon. The other is the domestic cat. The chameleon and the domestic cat are tacticians when it comes to a direct fight with snakes. As timid and small as these creatures are in relation to snakes they always win the fight.

The fight between a chameleon and a snake usually arises because of territorial disputes and hunting rights. The snake always provokes the chameleon. When this happens the chameleon remains calm and adapts to the fight by changing its colour to suit its environment. The snake would be up on its tail with its head flattened and hissing tongue protruding from its mouth in an 'I will kill you' posture. However, the chameleon being slow, watchful and a calculating planner concentrates on one goal, to send a dashing supersonic tongue lash to capture the snakes tongue.

The chameleon is capable of targeting and capturing its prey with its tongue up to a metre beyond its head position in a split second. So as the snake is trying to bite the chameleon, the calculating chameleon quietly estimates the distance to send a lightening attack right to the snakes' tongue. Unfortunately, although the snake is aware of this strategy it can do little about it because it cannot bite its enemy without engaging in a tongue exposing posture.

So the calculations by both sides go on and on until in a moment the chameleon attacks and tears off the tongue of the snake rendering it harmless. The fight ends because the snake without a tongue is harmless and unable to eject deadly poison. Moreover a snake without a tongue is bound to die due to the pain and bleeding inflicted by this action.

The domestic cat is yet another able contender for a title fight. The cat relies on its agility to keep away from the ferocious attacks of the snake by ducking left, right and backwards and using its claws to wad off possible close range attacks by the snake. At a moments notice when the snake pre-supposes that all is well, the cat leaps for the kill and grabs and rips off the snakes tongue. The fight is over.

Apart from the chameleon and the cat, people are perhaps snake's most sworn enemies. In the Christian faith the days of this enmity has divine origins. According to the bible the snake deceived Eve to eat the forbidden fruit in the Garden of Eden. When this happened God pronounced a curse upon the human race and people and snake became permanent enemies. God declared that from that time onwards the snake would bruise a person's heel and a person would shatter a snakes head. To this day whenever people see snakes, they will always attempt to kill them even without any provocation. This fight between people and snakes depends also on how poisonous the snake is. The more poisonous the snake is, the higher the chances of a fierce fight between a person and a snake. People will always initiate the fight in an attempt to eliminate the snake particularly when the snake is spotted near their dwelling. Two strategies for fighting snakes are used by people. Either it will be a direct face to face attack using missiles, like clubs and stones to smash the snakes' head or human beings will employ a simple capture technique to arrest the snake.

The skill of capturing live snakes using a Y shaped stick and a bag was known among several communities in time past. When a snake was spotted anywhere the first thing would be to corner it against a wall or object so that it cannot escape forcing it to turn and face its opponent. A Y shaped stick was then pushed into its open mouth as it positioned itself to attack. As the snake made frantic attempts to bite the stick, the Y shaped stick was sandwiched between its upper and lower jaws and it was quickly whisked into an open bag and rendered captive. The purpose of this was to rid snakes from people's immediate vicinity or to use the snakes for medicinal purposes by traditional healers or simply to rear the snakes. The captured snake also provided an easy and sure way of killing it since it could no longer escape.

Questions

1. Mention three fierce enemies of a snake.
2. Why does the fight between the snake and its enemies occur?
3. Describe how a snake is killed by each of its different enemies.
4. Explain how snakes are demobilized in this passage.
5. Describe the different fights between the snake and its enemies and the likely winner.

New words			
gigantic	audacity	tacticians	unleash
provokes	supersonic	posture	sandwiched
instincts	ferocious	duck	curse
bruise	provocation	eliminate	whisked

CHAPTER 3

The Flying Snake

In the plains of Tanzania the 'flying snake' is perhaps one of the most feared snake species. This is because, as opposed to the majority of snakes, which move on the ground, this snake attacks its victims by climbing trees and using tree branches as a springboard for its attacks. It bleats like a goat and is usually mistaken for a tethered goat calling for help in the fields.

The flying snake moves from branch to branch and from tree to tree among a cluster of nearby trees. Because of its speed only the sound of leaves is heard across the trees where it is passing. The sound it makes resembles the cha-cha-cha sound of a fast moving train. This sends great fear to anyone nearby because only the shaking of leaves is observed.

The flying snake moves to and fro this cluster of trees, which can be up to half a kilometer apart, declaring the whole of this region its territory. Any victim spotted below as it moves to and fro will have to face its wrath. Occasionally the flying snake will stop to take a rest. As it does so it bleats like a goat.

When the 'flying snake' spots a trespasser, it coils its tail on a branch of a tree and waits for its victim. When its victim unknowingly passes under the tree, it springs and strikes the victim's head with a deadly blow before retracting into the tree like an elastic rubber band. This is where the snake derives its name, it attacks so quickly that the villagers assume it actually flies.

To kill the 'flying snake', the villagers have devised an appropriate quick fix method. Due to the difficulty in getting close to the 'flying snake' the most important means for fighting it is to identify where it is by its conspicuous bleating and perhaps the history of its previous attacks. The most effective method is by using hot porridge. The porridge is boiled in a pot and a woman carries the hot porridge in an open pot on her head determined to pass under the trees where the 'flying snake' has been spotted. As soon as she is in the vicinity of the snake it attacks her by unleashing its split second strike aimed at biting the top of her head, but instead the 'flying snake' lands inside the boiling porridge and is scalded to death.

Questions

1. Explain the origin of the name 'flying snake'
2. What are some of the characteristics of the flying snake?
3. How is the flying snake different from other snakes?
4. Describe how the flying snake attacks its victims.
5. How do villagers kill the flying snake?

New Words			
species	cluster	trespasser	springboard
bleats	scalded	victims	unleashing
vicinity	tethered	retracting	conspicuous

CHAPTER 4

Why Cat is Not People's Best Friend

They say a dog is people's best friend because of its loyalty. A cat is not however peoples best friend. Even though a cat adds value to human lives in several ways, it is its overly zealous sense of duty that has cost it this friendship. In the rural traditional settings rodents are often a problem, constantly destroying harvested crops, stored in the homestead. It takes a cat to keep rats and mice at bay and protect people's resources from this economic plunder and wastage. However, an amazing account is told of how the cat led to men wearing trousers.

Long ago in Central Uganda the traditional dress for men was a long usually white towering cloth from shoulder to the feet called the "Kanzu". When this attire was draped on, the need for trousers and under wears was optional. Frequently many men did not wear trousers or under wears.

Legend has it that one particular evening an old man was by the fireside in his home enjoying the warmth of the fireplace. He was busy preparing a chicken meal which traditionally was a meal prepared and eaten by men only. His cat was also resting close by directly facing the master and curious at what the master was doing. The master slaughtered the hen, removed the feathers and proceeded to chop it up into small pieces. He then washed the chicken pieces and put them into the pot to boil. As custom has it he took some of the chicken pieces to roast and hopefully eat before the main meal was ready. Because of the seating position of the master the cat had a clear vision of what lay under the kanzu as he was busy preparing the meal.

When the master shifted on his chair his whole body moved and the cat thought she had spotted a rat move under the kanzu and paid close attention to try and map out a strategy of attacking and killing the rat. As the cat was contemplating what to do next the master again shifted his position to check on the chicken he was roasting and this made the cat hyperactive trying hard to secure an attacking position for the purported mannerless rat nearby. The master watched with curiosity and wondered why the cat was behaving strangely. When the master thought to rise up and get some salt within the room to add to his meal, the cat took a leap for the purported escaping rat. Loud was the yell of the master that the whole household came scrambling to find out what was happening only to find the cat tightly holding the master in the middle section where the purported rat had been sighted under the kanzu. No amount of shouting and yelling could persuade the cat to let go. The master in pain, pushed the cat's tail into the fire. The cat let go of its hold. The man was quickly rushed to a traditional healer and nursed for two weeks. Fortunately nothing was lost. To this day men wear trousers under their kanzus, just in case history repeats itself. And as for the cat, he always sits a safe distance away from people.

For the rich and superstitious, however, cats are loved because cats are reliable poison detectors. When a cat is offered poisoned food two things happen that are both instructive to people about the possibility of the food being poisoned. Legend has it that a cat will not eat food that contains poison and if forced to eat it, it would either die or show immediately the symptoms of poisoning. If the cat gladly obliges and eats the food, it suggests that the meal is fit for human consumption. It is said of many prominent people that whenever they were invited to unfamiliar places they would always apply the cat-eat-food-first test to determine whether to partake of the meal or not. Should the cat reject the food portion the cook is immediately summoned to carry out a public food test before the watchful eyes of all the people.

Questions

1. State three reasons why cat is man's friend.
2. Explain how a cat made man to wear under wears and trousers.
3. How does a cat attack and kill a rat.
4. Describe the behaviour of a cat when given poisoned food.
5. List the advantages of keeping cats in our homes.

New Words			
obliged	rodents	nuisance	prominent
plunder	draped	hyperactive	summon
purported	attire	contemplate	scrambling

CHAPTER 5

Deadly Leopards

The leopard is perhaps Africa's most subtle, agile and ferocious big cat. It is merciless, lethal and ruthless. Because leopards climb trees it is much more difficult for its victim to escape from them compared to the lion. It is often said that in the plains of semi-arid Karamoja in Uganda, when one meets a leopard resting on a low lying tree branch and he pretends that he has not seen the leopard then one is safe. Otherwise any abrupt reaction particularly when eye contact has been made results in a deadly attack.

The leopard is quite a voracious animal and often when it attacks domestic animals in a homestead it causes great loss by its modus operandi. When a leopard attacks a pen of domestic animals it first kills all of them and then settles to feast on only one animal.

The morning following a leopard attack the owner of the domestic animals would sound the war cry and all the strong young men would be gathered together armed with spears and clubs. They would then set off in search of the big cat, which was a risky venture. Sometimes they found the big cat and fought and killed it, with human casualties. Sometimes the young men could not locate the leopard and returned empty handed. However on return to the village a big meal was prepared from the carcasses left behind by the leopard. The entire village feasted and danced into the wee hours of the night.

The modus operandi of the leopard when it attacks man has been well corroborated as being identical. It always invariably tears off flesh from the back of the head to cover the face of man. In the days when hunting was a popular activity for the rural folk, the leopard inflicted the greatest damage to such hunting expeditions. No matter how many people were in the hunting team the leopard always attempted to attack them simultaneously injuring each of them. That meant if ten men were involved in a hunt and came across a leopard almost all the ten men would nurse leopard wounds if they were lucky enough to get away alive unless they were brave men and knew exactly the tactics required to demobilize the leopard. When rifles were later introduced the individual who held the rifle was in more danger because leopards have a death instinct and will attack anyone raising a rifle to take aim at them.

Questions

1. A Leopard is called a big cat. Mention other animals that are included in this group of big cats.
2. Why is a Leopard a very dangerous animal?
3. Give as much details of the behaviour of the Leopard.
4. Describe how a Leopard attacks domestic animals.
5. Explain what happens when a Leopard attacks people.

New words			
subtle	ferocious	ruthless	agile
voracious	carcass	demobilize	wee hours
modus operandi	corroborated	expedition	tactics
invariably	bravery	instinct	simultaneously

CHAPTER 6

Fighting Leopards—Part One

In time past among the Karamojong tribesmen of Uganda transition from boyhood to manhood involved hunting down and killing a leopard. When a Karamojong warrior kills a leopard he is elevated to manhood status and the privileges that come along with this is that he can now marry a woman and is accorded respect within the tribe. The evidence of this feat is that the warrior's left shoulder is tattooed with dot marks in the shape of a rectangle as a public testimony of his elevated position in the society.

Hunting and killing a leopard is not without risks yet it is a necessary feat among the Karamojong warriors. Despite the ferocity of the leopard the Karamojong warriors have been schooled in the art of fighting leopards. Karamoja is semi-desert and so the terrain is made up mainly of thorn shrubs as the predominant vegetation. To kill a leopard the intending warrior cuts a large branch of the thorn shrub. Armed with a spear and knife, he goes out into the Karamoja wilderness in search of the leopards during the day. This is the easiest time to win the battle as during the night when the leopards hunt for food they are very discrete, mobile and not easily visible to man. During day time the leopard would be found resting on low lying trees after a successful nights' hunting mission.

The warrior moves towards the tree and provokes the resting leopard while chanting a war song. In its rage the leopard makes a leap towards the invading warrior who then raises the thorn shrub towards the leopard whose claws are outstretched in an attacking posture. Its claws then get entangled in the thorn shrubs and the warrior quickly takes hold of its tail. Half the battle has been won provided the tail is securely held in the warrior's grip. The secret here is that the leopard, unlike a dog, has a continuous unsegmented backbone and cannot turn around when the tail is held. There is no way the leopard can get closer to the warrior holding its tail despite frantic attempts. The warrior and the leopard now begin to pace around with the warrior firmly holding the leopards' tail and the leopard looking for every opportunity to escape. When the leopard is tired the warrior draws his spear from his waistband and quickly plunges his spear into the leopards stomach. The warrior then reverts to hold the tail with both hands as the bleeding leopard now fights for dear life to free itself. After a short while the leopard bleeds to death and the fight is over.

A story my grandmother told me lends credence to the experience just narrated. This happened in another part of the country. In those days travel was on foot because there were no cars. One day a man and his wife set off to visit relations in another part of the countryside and as they traveled a whole days' journey it started getting dark whilst they were still a long way from their destination. Then unexpectedly it began to rain and this forced them to take shelter in an abandoned partly collapsed mud hut that they came across on their way.

Unknown to them was the fact that during the day this abandoned hut was used by a leopard and its two cubs. As the travellers sheltered quietly behind the door the leopard suddenly appeared from her hunting expedition clutching a rabbit in its mouth. It walked straight past the travelers to her cubs afar off at the other end of the hut. As soon as this happened the man sensing death did the most sensible thing: rather than run off and face the wrath of the leopard, he quickly grabbed the leopards' tail and a death-and-life struggle quickly ensued between them. When the leopard was tired the man stuck his spear into the leopard's stomach and continued to hold its tail till it died. He proceeded to skin the leopard for its prestigious and much sought after skin. He used this to pep up his account when he finally got to his destination. The point of this story was what must be done when one encounters a leopard: get to the leopard's tail before it gets to you!

The leopard skin is the most treasured possession of all animal skins as it symbolizes power, courage and fearlessness. Look around the chiefdoms of Africa, and all the paramount chiefs particularly of the so called 'warrior tribes' are draped in leopard skins, and not lion skins, as evidence of chieftainship. Why?

Questions

1. Who are the Karamojong and what lifestyle do they live?
2. Why do Karamojong hunt Leopards?
3. Describe how the Karamojong fight Leopards.
4. What risks are involved in hunting a Leopard?
5. Explain the significance of a Leopard skin.

New Words			
warrior	elevated	feat	tattooed
mobile	discrete	rage	frantic
treasure	paramount	draped	clutching
wrath	ferocity	pace	prestigious

CHAPTER 7

Fighting Leopards—Part Two

Among the Masai warriors of Tanzania and Kenya the philosophy of killing a leopard is quite different from that of the Karamojong warriors. Fearlessness involves a face-to-face battle.

The Masai are pastoralists and keep hundreds of herds, which they graze in the same habitat as that of the wild animals. Their traditional weapons are spears, shields and clubs. It is worth noting that the Masai never throw spears at an opponent but instead use their spears for stubbing in short-range direct combat. The Masai shields are made from very strong animal hides and are jokingly referred to as bulletproof armour.

Because a leopard is a much smaller animal than a lion and much swifter and more lethal in attack the Masai use a special Y-shaped stick to fight it. To the Masai warrior the leopard skin is very valuable and is required intact without any perforations caused by a spear. The use of the spear is ruled out. The Masai kill a leopard with a club. A Y shaped stick is used by the warriors as they provoke the leopard into a fight. As the leopard leaps to attack the warrior uses the shield for protection from the claws of the leopard and simultaneously positions the stick to trap its neck to keep the leopard under control. A club is used to constantly hit the leopard's head.

If the leopard disentangles itself from the hold of the Y-shaped stick the warrior re-positions the stick using the shield for protection. If the leopard leaps at him, he wads off the attack with the Y-shaped stick to hold its neck and slow its forward motion while lashing blows on its head with his club. The head injuries result in death without ever damaging the skin, which is a precious possession to the warriors.

Questions

1. Name the weapons the Masai use to hunt Leopards.
2. Why do the Masai kill Leopards?
3. What are the differences between the Karamojong and Masai in fighting Leopards.
4. Describe the use of a Y shaped stick by the Masai in fighting Leopards.
5. Compare and contrast the Karamojong and Masai methods of fighting Leopards.

New words

demobilize	perforations	combat	habitat
disentangle	opponent	armour	frantic
simultaneously	unsegmented	philosophy	lethal

CHAPTER 8

Lion King of the Jungle

Long, long ago lions roamed the great expanse of the African wilderness. However with the passage of time population pressures caused people to compete for the vast resource that once formed the natural habitat of animals. Also the introduction of modern technology like sophisticated weapons led to the decimation of the animal species. A lion is perhaps one of the most predictable wild animals when it comes to its public relations with people. In an encounter with a lion the chances of survival are much higher particularly when the lion has had a good meal. In Karamoja it is said lions and people share the same paths without conflict. When a lion sees a warrior walking towards it, it simply turns off the path to the nearest tree, and lies down facing the intruder who must continue along the same path and show no visible signs of panic in order to be safe. When this happens the lion returns to the path and continues its journey.

My grandmother once narrated to me that when my aunt was a baby, she left the house early in the morning to cultivate her nearby garden carrying baby aunt on her back. She gently put down the baby in the shade and got on to her business of working her garden. No sooner did she raise her head than she saw a lion standing by her baby. She stared in disbelief as the lion also stared at her. The pain of child bearing could not allow her to just abandon her daughter and ran. So she summoned courage, walked towards the lion and picked up her baby and fled home. Strangely the lion did not move. When my breathless grandmother had narrated her ordeal, a few armed men returned to the scene but found the lion had left. They collected my grandmother's hoe and some of the baby clothes that had dropped in panic and returned home. The lion would have been allowed to live but for one grave error: it attacked cows grazing nearby. There was a trumpet call to summon the entire community to the presence of the predator in the village. The young men quickly mobilized, fought and killed the lion. My grandmother says she felt she should have repaid that lion by protecting it, but how could she convince these young men baying for its blood?

It is said that when a human being gets attacked by a lion then either it has been provoked, for instance by intruding into its privacy especially when it has cubs. Alternatively, it may attack a person as a strategic manouvre to get rid of the human being for its own purposes, as in the case of a herdsman who must be removed before the lion can prey on the domestic animals.

Also it is usually lions weakened by age that attack human beings since they cannot hunt for food.

Lions do not climb trees except for low-lying braches of say fallen trees. However they have a way of bringing down prey that has taken cover up in the high branches of a tree. The lion will urinate on its tail and spray the urine to where the opponent is. The effect of this is that once the urine gets into contact with the opponent it causes lethargic itching resulting in the prey falling down to the waiting lion.

Questions

1. Why are lions considered predictable and not very dangerous to man.
2. Explain the factors that threaten the existence of lions.
3. What are the advantages of lions moving together as a group?
4. How do lions deal with opponents who have climbed trees?
5. Compare and contrast the characteristics of a leopard and that of a lion.

New words			
technology	conflict	mobilized	cubs
sophisticated	intruder	privacy	habitat
manouvre	panic	predictable	abandon
lethargic	survival	summon	strategic

CHAPTER 9

Lions Hunting Food

Lions are communal animals and stick together for life activities especially during hunting and feeding. One lion cannot hunt effectively as it is no match for some animals like zebra or antelope in a speed or a power contest. It is said that the blow from a zebras' hind legs is capable of breaking the jaws of a lion.

To hunt, a group of lions would first determine the wind direction by using their front feet to scoop the soil on the ground to produce dust and assess the direction of the wind. This is very necessary because the scent of lions carried by the wind is recognized by animals afar off resulting in them running away to safety.

The lions then send one of their own to the water hole where all animals congregate to drink water very early in the morning or late in the evening. At the same time the rest of the group takes up ambush positions around the waterhole in a direction away from where the wind is blowing so as not to be spotted by the other animals. The lion by the water hole would then give off the characteristic Lion King of the jungle roar which would cause the panic-ridden animals to scamper off for dear life. The lions in ambush positions would then locate suitable prey coming their way and spring onto their back immediately bringing them down while sinking their teeth on their necks. They would congregate and share the meal collectively with the older members having their fill first and the young cubs last.

Sometimes when slow moving prey is met the group of lions attack it from all directions. The sharp incessant bites to the hind legs and neck of the animal results in its complete immobility. For a large slow moving animal like the giraffe one of the lions jumps on its back with its claws firmly embedded into its neck. The animal falls to the ground where the other lions proceed to help in the attack and kill it for their meal.

The lion, affectionately called the king of the jungle is not without its own troubles. Amongst these troubles is when attacked by a pack of wild dogs. This is perhaps the dreaded fight any lion would want to be engaged in. The wild dogs fight as a gang. When they come across a lone lion they encircle it and while barking and howling will bite the lion from both the rear and the front. Some of the wild dogs will bite the lion's tail and hind legs. While others are simply dodging the lion's claws keeping the lion occupied frantically trying to disengage itself from the pack. When desperate the lion may even seek help from people to free itself from these masquerading enemies.

Questions

1. List the animals that lions prefer to hunt.
2. What effect does a lion's scent have on other animals, and how does this affect it?
3. Describe how lions hunt and kill their prey.
4. Suggest reasons why a single old lioness might die of starvation.
5. Explain how a pride of lions would attack a large animal like an elephant successfully.

New words			
communal	scamper	incisors	contest
prey	embedded	scent	congregate
spring	pride	ambush	incessant

CHAPTER 10

The Love Potion

A story is told about a wealthy woman who visited a traditional medicine man seeking for a love potion. It was for her husband, so that he could love her more. The husband and his wife were having disagreements and their marriage had reached a crisis point. The traditional medicine man prescribed a potion that had to be mixed with milk from a lioness. The woman was told to go and bring milk from a lioness before the traditional medicine man could provide her with the concoction.

Desirous of mending her relationship with her husband the woman located a lioness with cubs and befriended it. She walked to where the lioness was nursing her cubs with chunks of meat everyday for several days feeding it. The lioness was cautious about the food being provided but helped herself to it and gave some to her cubs. This continued for several days, until the woman became a familiar sight to the lioness. Each time she saw the woman she ran towards her expecting the arrival of food. As time passed by the lioness did not only eat the food but also rubbed herself against the woman in a friendly manner.

As the lioness rubbed herself against the woman she would gently scratch its back and the lioness felt calmed. They developed a cordial relationship to an extent that they would run up and down as the feeding progressed and the lioness would rub herself against the woman who in response would scratch her back. The lioness appeared to enjoy this unique friendship, which continued for a long time with the woman.

Every time she visited the lioness and her cubs with meat chunks, she carried a cup and took drops of milk from the lioness. The lioness did not seem to mind the taking of the milk. On the day the woman succeeded in taking sufficient milk from the lioness for the medicine man, she did not return to the lioness again. She rushed to the traditional medicine man who asked to be briefed on how she had succeeded. The traditional medicine man then went ahead to give his prescription by saying to the woman 'Just as you have been patient and successful in milking a lioness, extend the same patience to your husband'. The woman left the traditional medicine man's house highly disappointed and complaining "this is shear nonsense. I should have been killed by this lioness. You are a wretched medicine man". However, the trick worked for the woman and her marriage succeeded.

Questions

1. Why did the woman visit a medicine man and what advice was she given.

2. Describe the steps the woman took to milk a lioness.

3. Why did the lioness not mind about this unique friendship?

4. What risks did the woman undergo in accomplishing the task of milking a lioness.

5. Why was the woman successful?

New words			
potency	chunk	cubs	concoction
unique	incident	thrilled	prescription
cautiously	accomplishment	mare	potion

CHAPTER 11

Hunting Down Hyenas

Whenever you see lions feasting, hyenas are always nearby keeping watch because they are assured of a meal that entails all the leftovers of the carcass. A hyena is an animal with very powerful forelegs yet a great coward to the marrow. Before a hyena can settle down to any food it comes across it first determines whether the carcass is dead or alive. It stands afar off and then runs at full speed close to the intended meal it has spotted. This is done several times and if no movement is sensed it assumes the target is either dead or harmless. It then summons courage to get close to the intended meal.

Hyenas are greedy animals. They often make unwise choices. Once upon a time, so goes the story, Mr. Hyena was traveling along a road, which suddenly ran into a T-junction, with one road going left and the other going right. Mr. Hyena looked left then right and thought to himself, if I go left I may find food, but if I go right I may as well find food. So he decided to go left, but after traveling a short while he stopped and returned to the junction and preceded right thinking perhaps there were better opportunities that side. After much running in this direction with no visible signs of food he stopped abruptly and changed direction to go back to the left where he had just come from. Because there was no food in sight he returned to the other side. This continued for the whole night with Mr. Hyena travelling to and fro on an empty stomach and eventually collapsed due to fatigue and hunger.

In the olden days hyenas used to dwell close to human settlements by the rocks of Nyero in Ngora in Eastern Uganda and at night they made weird sounds. The presence of hyenas posed a real danger to the goats and sheep that the people kept. This led to a deliberate attempt to eliminate the hyena species from within the vicinity of people's houses.

However because of the hyena's fearful disposition they were hard to come by so people devised an impressive strategy. Hyenas were regular visitors to people's dwelling places at night when everybody was asleep. People dug deep holes in the ground where they would place large water pots and cover the pots up completely, except the pots' mouth. At the bottom of the water pot, offal's and meat were placed as bait and the pot was then filled up completely to the brim with water.

In the darkness of the night the hyenas would spot the scent of the offal's and meat and would try everything within their power to get to the bottom of the pot so as to retrieve and eat the offal's and meat. Invariably the only option thinkable would be to first drink all the water before getting to the offal's and meat at the bottom of the pot. They would drink and drink and drink and sometimes they would succeed in emptying the pot of water. This was a difficult task that was often abandoned. When the hyenas had their stomachs full of water, a trumpet was sounded by the watchful villagers to gather the young men. They would hunt the hyenas down. Sometimes the water was mixed with traditional brew, which made the hyenas drunk and start laughing loudly. This was how their presence was detected in the village and the young men would then mobilize and attack them. In a drunken state the hyenas never made any attempt to run away.

Questions

1. Why are hyenas called greedy animals?
2. Describe the lifestyle of a hyena.
3. Why are hyenas a threat near people's dwelling?
4. How were hyenas killed in time past.
5. Narrate any story about hyenas that you have heard about.

New words			
mobilize	carcass	bellies	weird
disposition	eliminate	vicinity	retrieve deliberate
bait	ovals	fatigue	

CHAPTER 12

Pythons in Action

In my native Teso land pythons are quite common and usually dwell in anthills. During the mango season, around April to June each year young boys gather mangoes in the nearby bushes and encounters with pythons are quite common. Several years ago when I was on a mango-gathering mission I climbed a mango tree, which had an anthill at its foot. Unknown to me was the fact that this was the dwelling of a huge python. No sooner did we start enjoying the fruits with other boys than a fearful looking python emerged from the anthill and made attempts to climb the same tree we were in.

We were terribly frightened at this big snake attempting to climb the tree we were in. Immediately we all started to scream as the snake continuously raised its head above its body and wagged its tongue as if looking for a victim to attack. Mesmerized by the size of this creature we held on to the tree branches and continued to scream as the snake slowly made its way out of the anthill and made frantic attempts to climb the tree. Our screams were answered by an approaching barking dog. This caused the snake to now steadily climb up the tree trunk and we knew it was time to find our way out. We fled from the tree branches and dived to the ground like soldiers escaping a military ambush and settled for a 'sprint for life race' only remembering to nurse our injuries later when the danger was averted. On reaching home and explaining our ordeal to our parents they recognized the big snake as a python.

The python is perhaps the biggest and longest reptile in the snake family. The python is a shy animal, which hunts and kills its prey in a very fascinating manner. Its preys include rabbits, hares, birds and sometimes goats and on rare occasions it attacks human beings. When a python spots its prey it overpowers it by coiling itself around it. The shock of this act leaves the prey paralyzed and unable to free itself. It exerts a force on the prey to squeeze life out of it.

When the prey is dead, it secretes saliva onto it until the whole carcass is smooth and then swallows it. After this the python hibernates in the bush for many days until the whole carcass is completely digested in its stomach. The python now becomes part of the vegetation and is completely unrecognizable as it takes several days for digestion to be complete. Usually in this state it is mistaken for a log by women collecting firewood in the bushes. Any attempt to use an axe to split the python thinking it is a piece of log has no effect on the python. The skin is so tough that the axe rebounds without effect, no matter how sharp.

When attacked by a python and overpowered, there is just one remedy to free oneself. After it has entangled round you and exerted its force to squeeze life out of you, aim for the tail, and bite it as hard as you could. The pain caused by your grip on its delicate tail brings the desired freedom. It will relax its squeeze and the shock you get is that you will be thrown far away as the python disentangles itself from your body and escapes.

Questions

1. How do pythons kill their prey?
2. What happens when a python has swallowed a rabbit?
3. How does one escape from being killed by a python?
4. Describe a python in your own words.
5. Narrate what you would do if a python climbed up the tree you were in.

New words			
prey	reptile	fascinating	subsequently
hibernates	gravity	paralyzed	delicate
carcass	disentangles	digested	rebounds
digestion	mesmerized	frantic	ambush

CHAPTER 13

The Kind Gorillas

It was early morning in a village called Luwero in Uganda where peasants were busy tending their coffee farms like they had done over the years. However, today was to be a different day in the history of the village. Staccato gunfire tik . . . tik . . . tik . . . tik rocked the otherwise peaceful village as peasants scampered for shelter in the thick forests. Why all the shooting? This was the question in the minds of the scared villagers. Was it government soldiers, was it rebel infiltrators, was it armed thieves, no answers were forthcoming as survival dictated escape first and questions later. As families fled for shelter children were left on their own, the whole saga lasted the whole morning and afternoon and by this time the village was completely deserted with peasants trekking far away for safety.

However, for Namutebi this was to be a day not to be forgotten in her life. Having just given birth to her first baby boy six months earlier, she was quite happy taking care of the young infant as a single mother living with her parents. On this fateful day she woke up as usual. After feeding her son, they both left for the coffee farm. She was going to weed the bush around the coffee trees. She gently laid down her son in a swaddle of clothes on the ground as she always did and started clearing the bushes. Little did she know that this was to be the last time she would ever see her son.

As the shooting started and confusion broke out the whole village fled in panic. Namutebi took cover behind the coffee trees as the gunfire increased in intensity. She then bolted off without ever thinking about the little boy cuddled in clothes nearby. It was only after she had traveled to safety that she remembered leaving her son lying on the ground near where she was working. A sudden fear for her son gripped her. She stopped to consider that the only option she had was to return and collect her child amidst fears. Although gunfire was still ringing in her village, she decided to brave it and save her baby but was restrained by the villagers. It was practically impossible to do anything than to offer prayers for the life of her infant baby. Later in the evening the village was quiet and Namutebi with a group of villagers ventured back into the village. When they reached the spot where she had earlier left her baby the infant was nowhere to be found. They searched all the bushes around and every bit of shrub but to no avail. Frantic efforts over the next few days were made to locate the child but were fruitless.

It is thought that as soon as the shooting subsided and the gunmen had left, the baby started to cry as a result of hunger, thirst and over exposure to the elements of nature. This forced a colony of gorillas that was resting on the branches of the nearby trees to investigate the ordeal of the little unattended baby lying below where they were returning from the confusion that had rocked the village. The incessant cry of the baby attracted the sympathy of the gorillas who immediately came over the deserted patch of land picked up the baby and started feeding it with wild fruits and gave it water to drink. This was the beginning of a friendship that lasted about four years with the gorilla colony. The little baby became part of the gorilla stable being fed, protected and assimilated into their way of life as they moved through the dense African forest.

Five years later, a war of liberation was quickly gaining momentum in the vicinity of Namutebi's village, which was not far away from the capital city. Troops were marching towards the city in an effort to capture power from the incumbent regime and as they cut their way through the bushes they came across a colony of defiant gorillas, which was persuaded to flee by a barrage of gunfire. However something strange was in the offing that afternoon as the troops watched the gorillas in flight. The last of its members was different from the rest of them and could not move as fast and moreover its climbing ability was limited. It looked human yet there is no doubt it was in the company of the gorilla colony.

Captain Juma, the commander of the mercenary force quickly took his binoculars and focused in the direction of the primates and as soon as he had made his assessment blew the whistle loosely hanging around his neck. Soon a group of battle hardened soldiers filed around him and instructions were given to radio other troops around this area. They were to capture alive the last member of the gorilla colony as soon as possible. Within two hours the chase was over and the pseudo gorilla member had been safely apprehended. It turned out that this was a pseudo guerilla—a human being yet behaving like a guerilla. Captain Juma was baffled and quickly gave orders for "Saba-saba" as he had been nicknamed to be kept in safe custody until they found an asylum for him after the conquest of the capital.

In the next few days the battle for the city was accomplished and Saba-saba was taken to the children's' orphanage. However looking after this child was not easy. Often times he yelled like a guerilla and walked on all fours. In the dormitory he jumped from bed to bed and ate with both hands like a gorilla. Moreover at this age of about five years the child could not communicate in a meaningful language. It took a team of medical experts and counselors from the nearby hospital to carefully map out a strategy of integrating this child into society. What would you have done? All said and done, the good news is that Saba-saba has been integrated into normal life and is now pursuing university education courtesy of the gorillas and thanks to the government. Who knows what Saba-saba will become in future and his policy towards gorillas.

Questions

1. Explain the circumstances that led to the villagers of Luwero fleeing from their village and what were the consequences for Namutebi?
2. Describe how the colony of gorillas was able to take Namutebi's little baby boy.
3. Explain how Saba-Saba lived with the gorillas for about four years.
4. How was Saba-saba rescued?
5. What problems were faced in teaching Saba-Saba to live as a human being?

New words

staccato	saga	yelled	infiltrators
colony	peasants	mercenary	frantic
ordeal	swaddle	assimilated	asylum
incessant	dictated	incumbent	integration
orphanage	cuddled	barrage	offing
primates	scampered	stable	liberation
subsided	fateful	momentum	vicinity
persuaded	defiant	apprehended	ventured

CHAPTER 14

A Buffalo Hunt

Buffalo herds in the wild maintain and respect authority amongst them. The strongest male buffalo leads the entire herd and makes decisions about where to graze, which water points to patronize, which enemies to fight and which enemies to flee from and so on. Occasionally there are leadership contests among the buffaloes. An aspiring challenger would take on the reigning buffalo leader in a fierce fight under the watchful eyes of the entire herd. The buffalo to buffalo fight is a locked horn fight and at the end of the day each contestant may have lost part of their horns, not to name the body injuries sustained by continuous pushing and goring of each other. The loser is driven away from the main herd to start his own small herd together with a few disgruntled female buffalos.

Hunting a buffalo using spears is a traditionally perfected art. The buffalo is very dangerous usually goring its victims to death using its horns. It will use its horns to corner its victim against a tree or anthill and repeatedly gore the victim to death. Funny enough a buffalo never steps on its fallen victim with its feet preferring to jump over the victim instead. Hunters make use of these two facts.

Because buffalos graze together in a herd the traditional hunters first isolate one member from the herd of buffaloes, usually the one grazing at the outskirts of the main herd. This is done by approaching the buffalo, and whistling to attract its attention and when it attacks the intruder he quickly drops to the ground so that the buffalo cannot hurt him. Remember this is done in a chosen area where there are no nearby trees or anthills so as to protect the hunter from being gored. When the buffalo tries to use its horns to lift up the hunter he willingly rolls on the ground and immediately the next hunter emerges and draws the attention of the buffalo, which then charges at the second intruder. This process continues until the buffalo is lured to a safe distance away from the danger posed by the main buffalo herd.

When the buffalo is isolated from the herd, one of the hunters provokes the buffalo and when it charges at him he falls to the flat ground devoid of trees or anthills so that he cannot be gored. The buffalo attacks him as it gets closer and uses its horns to lift up the hunter. The hunter obliges and rolls on the ground. As this is taking place the second hunter emerges and quickly thrashes his spear into the buffalos belly and runs away. The buffalo's attention now shifts to this second hunter and madly rushes for him and as it nears him this second hunter falls to the ground. The buffalo again attempts to gore him against a tree or anthill or uneven ground surface and his escape is to keep rolling as the horns push him on the ground. The first hunter now appears as the attention of the buffalo is on the second hunter lying on the ground and also thrashes his spear into the buffalo and the same cycle repeats itself. This continues until the buffalo eventually succumbs to death.

Buffalo meat is really tasty especially if dried and cooked in groundnut soup. The meat tears off in shreds and eeh, I tell you there is nothing tasty like that. Traditional hunters always rate buffalo meat top and buffalos are number one target in any hunting expedition no matter the danger posed.

A buffalo is friend to domestic livestock and usually if a buffalo joins a herd of domestic livestock friendship is quickly forged such that they graze together and nest together. The buffalo is normally recognized by its towering size above that of the ordinary cows. It was not uncommon among the Iteso tribesmen of Uganda to wake up early in the morning and quickly rush off to the kraal to take the cows to graze and find buffalo among them. The surprise guest caused the herdsman to escape as fast as his legs could carry him.

It is surprising that despite the fearfulness of buffaloes in Africa, in India buffaloes are domesticated and used to plough the land in preparation for the planting of crops. They are preferred to oxen because they are much stronger. Usually to plough a field two buffaloes are yoked together and driven along the furrows as they pull the plough. We hope that one day the buffaloes of Africa will also be tamed to provide agricultural labour to people.

Questions

1. Mention some similarities and some differences between buffaloes and cows.
2. Describe how a buffalo kills its victim.
3. Explain how a buffalo is traditionally hunted and killed.
4. Why do two male buffaloes occasionally fight and what are the results.
5. What two facts do hunters use in killing a buffalo?

New words			
obliges	succumbs	herd	gore
provokes	isolate	thrashes	shreds
outskirts	expedition	reigning	disgruntled
towering	patronize	contests	challenger
aspiring	fierce	towering	domesticated

CHAPTER 15

Cattle Rustling in Action

Cattle rustling involves a group of warriors raiding another village or community and forcefully taking their livestock usually cattle, goats, sheep, donkeys, horses and camels. This is carried out by especially the Karamojong warriors on the neighbouring communities of the Teso, Bagisu, Sebei and Langi of Uganda and the Turkana of Kenya. It is actually aggravated armed robbery for the main purpose of raising dowry so one can marry. For a long time cattle rustling has continued and continues to occupy a large part of life among the Karamojong and other nomadic pastoralists of East Africa. However, with time the level of sophistication has changed from spears to home made guns to modern day rifles

Cattle rustling plays an important part among these nomadic pastoralists where traditional values have put much pressure on its members to continue the practice despite modernization and government effort to stop the practice. Long ago each Karamojong family kept hundreds of different animal herds. Cattle, goats and sheep were kept for meat, milk and blood. Camels were primarily kept for transport and also for meat and milk whilst donkeys were used for transport and farming activities. However, due to over grazing as a result of population growth and natural calamities such as drought the herds dwindled over time and today the livestock population has tremendously decreased. Unfortunately the demand by culture on having large herds has not eased.

To marry and be accorded a respectable status among the Karamojong, dowry in the form of a large herd of livestock has to be paid. However because of the limited animal population in the region the militaristic option has continued to dominate the life of the Karamojong. Livestock must be stolen from the neighbours to pay for the bride price and also to maintain the status quo of families.

Before a group of warriors embarks on a raid to the neighbouring tribes they congregate together in the vast plains away from their settlements with their weapons usually spears, clubs and home made guns. They plan where the raid is going to take place. They then send spies to check out the terrain, the availability of livestock and the strengths of their targeted neighbours. This expedition usually lasts several days because the warriors sent to spy the land walk several hundreds of kilometers. When word is brought back that livestock has been spotted there is a frenzy among the warriors no matter the dangers involved. That night weapons are polished and sharpened and pleasantries are exchanged because of the excitement of impending wealth to pay for the bride price.

A traditional medicine man is consulted about the outcome of the raid and his blessings and directions are the final phase of the start of a raiding expedition. The wages of the traditional medicine man that throws bones to direct the raiders on how to approach the village is a portion of the livestock after a successful raid.

The long trek begins the next day and takes several days before they arrive at the border with their neighbours since the journey is made on foot. When they are within reach of the village to be raided they spend the day before the attack resting and preparing for the night attack. On the night of the attack immediately after sun set the warriors zero into the village identified for the raid and take strategic positions.

The leader of the raid shoots into the air from his home made rifle signaling the commencement of the raid. Throughout the raid he continues to blow a whistle fastened around his neck to keep the warriors informed of his whereabouts and as a guide to the collective location of the warriors. The warriors then quickly rush off to the kraals where the livestock have been kept for the night opening and driving the livestock to an agreed assembly point. As soon as the sound of gunfire rocks the air there is confusion in the village with men, women and children fleeing in all directions for their lives. Houses are set ablaze and anyone found in the vicinity of the village is captured, shot or hacked to death. Often times it happens that in some of the villages raided some villagers possess guns and 'fire replies fire' as a battle for supremacy ensues. The Karamojong are known to be capable of shooting while hiding under the belly of a cow used as transport which they grasp tightly as they drive the cows. This means that they are not visible to their opponents. They cannot therefore be easily harmed while they are capable of much destruction.

A home made gun is made locally by traditional iron mongers and is only capable of firing one shot at a time. The barrel of the home made gun is cut short so that the gun makes a distinctive sound which the warriors recognize as their own ammunition in contrast to enemy fire.

Sometimes after the gun has fired several rounds of ammunition it becomes very hot so that it has to be left to cool down which is quite risky in the heat of battle. Cooling down of a homemade gun is important if target accuracy is to be maintained. Heat causes expansion of the metal barrel. When this occurs the gun can no longer maintain its shooting accuracy despite a good aim. Any further use of such a gun results in wasted ammunition.

The end of a raid is signaled by the peculiar blowing of the whistle by the leader of the raiders. Immediately all the raiders cut short any pending kraal operations and run back towards the direction where the whistle sound is coming from and the journey back to their homeland commences.

Home guards have been armed and deployed by the government to keep cattle rustling under control. However because of the surprise attack on a village and the vastness of the border with the Karamojong, the home guards cannot respond immediately. Often when they do respond the Karamojong warriors are on their way driving the raided herds back towards their settlements. Sometimes the home guards are successful in recovering the animals from the raiders but sometimes they are not successful. This mainly depends on their numbers in comparison to the raiders involved and the firepower at their disposal.

In contrast to the warriors, home guards use semi-automatic rifles. These guns are capable of firing up to ten shots of ammunition in rapid succession before they are re-loaded. The lack of tact of the warriors has often led to great success by the home guards in defeating them. When an armed warrior is shot dead, fellow warriors will never let go of his gun. A fellow warrior with a spear will immediately rush to pick up the dead warriors gun, no matter the risk involved. All that the home guard does is to concentrate on the spot where the dead warriors gun is, and keep shooting dead all the warriors attempting to pick up the dead warriors gun until he runs out of ammunition. It is not uncommon to fall down about ten other warriors attempting to recover a single rifle from a demobilized warrior.

The return journey by the raiders is a destructive one as the animals are driven very fast and through farmland destroying crops. The raiders also harvest crops in the field to carry along with them. If the raid was orchestrated by both the need for livestock and food then the raiders come along with women. When the men are busy assembling the livestock together the women would be involved in collecting food from the homesteads, which they carry back with them.

Sometimes because of the vastness of the terrain men and women captured during the raid are taken as captives to show the raiders the way they should go as they hurriedly exit the village. However when all is clear the captives are set free and have to trek several kilometers back to their village.

On reaching their settlements the animals are divided in an agreed format. First the medicine man is rewarded for his consultations followed by the young men who masterminded the raid. Finally the rest of the team in the raiding expedition receives an animal or two each. Other bachelor warriors in the raiding expedition now wait their turns for another successful raid to pay for bride price, since it involves teamwork.

Questions

1. Why do Karamojong warriors steal animals from their neighbours?
2. How is a raiding expedition planned?
3. Describe how a cattle raid is carried out.
4. Who are home guards and what do they do.
5. What risks do warriors face when on a raid?

New words			
frenzy	calamities	trek	modernization
terrain	dowry	supremacy	sophistication
dwindled	status-quo	iron-mongers	ammunition
orchestrated	pleasantries	nomadic	militaristic
expedition	masterminded	consultations	congregate

www.ingramcontent.com/pod-product-compliance
Lightning Source LLC
Chambersburg PA
CBHW020401290526
45785CB00005B/2390